LOYALIST MURALS

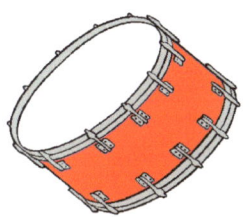 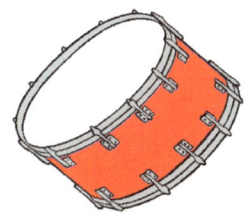

The following photographs are property of Aisling photography and Kevin Traynor

Aisling Photography Publishing

Belfast

www.aislingphotography.co.uk

Kevin Traynor asserts the moral right to be identified as the author of this work.
loyalist Murals of Northern Ireland 2008

ISBN 978-0-9556950-1-8

All rights reserved. No part of this publication may be reproduced, stored in a retrieval system, or transmitted, in any form or by any means, electronic, mechanical, photocopying, recording or otherwise, without the prior permission of the publishers.

YOUNG CITIZEN VOLUNTEERS

YCV

21-6-79 — 23-8-00

VOL. SAM ROCKETT

1 BATT — B COY

AT THE GOING DOWN OF THE SUN AND IN THE MORNING WE WILL REMEMBER HIM
HERE LIES A SOLDIER

MURDERED BY COWARDS

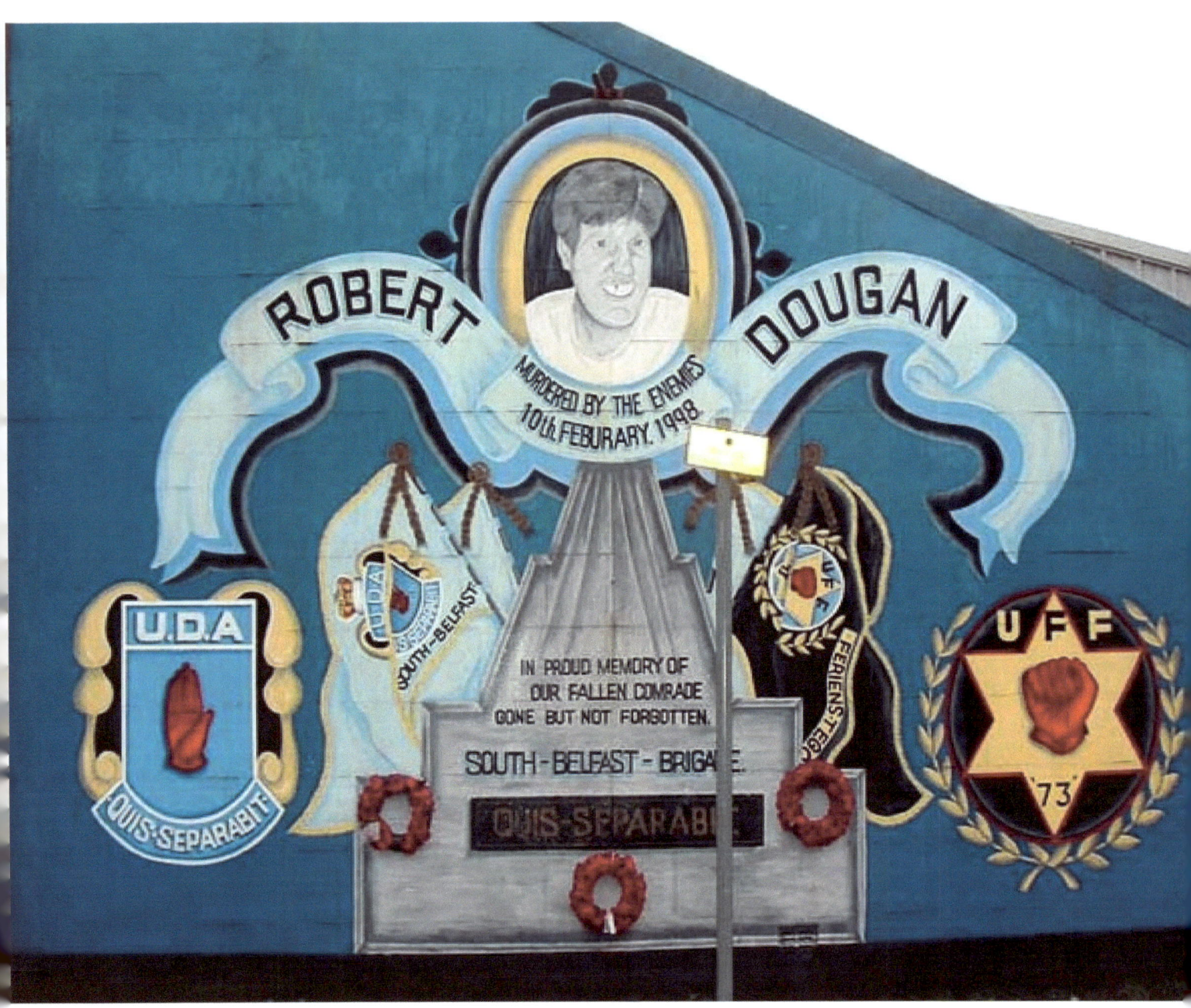

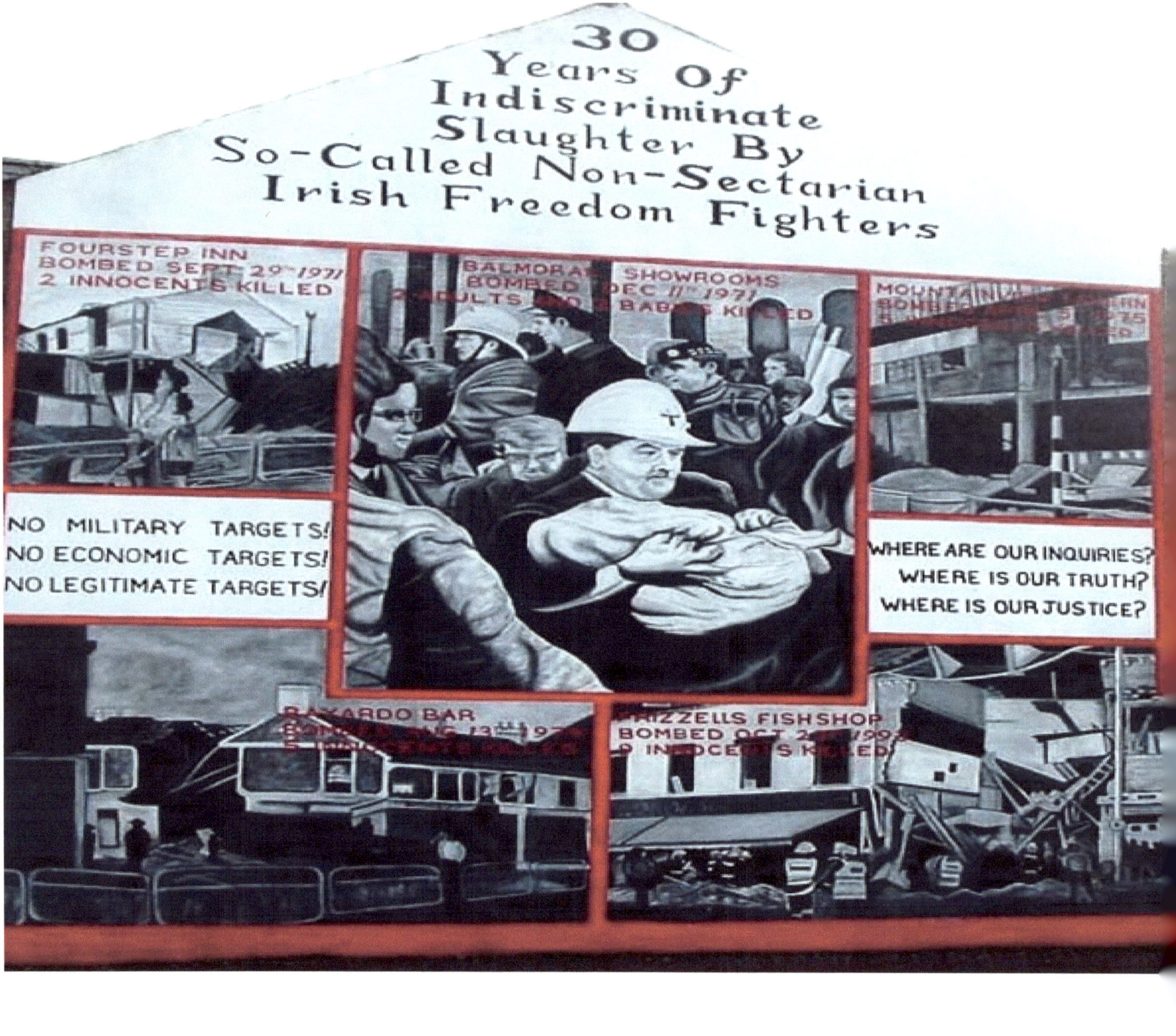

- This book has been produced by Kevin Traynor of Aisling Photography. For more information about Aisling Photography, why not contact us at www.aislingphotography.co.uk where more great Belfast images are available to look at and buy. Hope you enjoyed the book. Thanks.

This book features images from the following locations - Shankhill Road, Newtonards Road, Carrickfergus, Bangor, Mount Vernon, Roden Street, Templemore Avenue, Canada Street, Woodvale, Cregagh, Castlereagh, Rathcoole, Londonderry, The Village, Tigers bay, Sandy Row, Ballymacarret and Ballybeen.

www.ingramcontent.com/pod-product-compliance
Lightning Source LLC
Chambersburg PA
CBHW042017150426
43197CB00002B/59